# Seat-of-the-Pants Suppers

How to Cook for Those You Love When
All You Want to Do Is Sit Down and
Eat Already

by
Nancy Heiser

Illustrated by Charlotte Agell

Published by:

**Zipline Press**

P. O. Box 622
Brunswick, Maine 04011
www.ziplinepress.com

Additional copies may be ordered from the above address or
website.

Layout and design by Nancy Heiser.
Cover and illustrations by Charlotte Agell.

Printed in the United States of America.
First printing, 2001.

Seat-of-the-pants Suppers.

ISBN 0-9709259-0-5

Library of Congress Control Number: 2001088452

10 9 8 7 6 5 4 3 2 1

# Acknowledgements

Most people who cook have a few favorite simple-to-prepare, gotta-get-it-on-the-table meals in their arsenal. I extend my thanks to those friends and family members who contributed their recipes to this book. Wherever possible, I have mentioned the source of a recipe.

All the suppers included in this book were tested at home on my husband and children, who graciously ate whatever I put in front of them and occasionally offered suggestions for recipe improvements. I thank Dodie Jones and Liz Pierson who assisted with recipe testing. Liz also edited the manuscript. Thanks go to Renee Chevalier for her computer wizardry and to Kerry Leichtman and Paula Boyer Rougny for their helpful advice. I dedicate this book to Jeff, Dan, and Jillian, great supper companions. I might also mention that Shep, our Shetland sheepdog, always made sure the floor got clean of any spillage.

# Contents

# Introduction

The great mass of women and men work hard all day and come home to find that the fairy godmother has not descended upon the household to cook supper while they were out. These same people, tired and hungry themselves, cringe when they hear their children ask: "When's dinner?" or "Why can't we have pizza again?"

You may be one of these desperate people. You lead a busy life with many demands — holding a job, shuttling kids to after school activities, taking care of an elderly relative, cleaning up after the hamster. Putting together a home-cooked meal that is healthy, fast, and something the whole clan will enjoy is a continual challenge. You eat a lot of pizza or take-out. A typical side dish is a plastic bag of carrots. This book is for households like yours.

Let me tell you what this book is not. It is not for Julia Child wannabees. It does not attempt to compete with Martha Stewart. It is for those who want to get supper together quickly and without much fuss. It is food preparation that is quick, surgical, and sometimes irreverent. It is for the time-stressed and independent-minded cook. It is attack-the-kitchen cooking. The point is good food with the least amount of time and effort. Get the job done and move on. This book is for people who want to skip lengthy cookbook instructions and cut to the chase.

Are there recipes for the gourmand in this book? You won't find duck pate or chocolate torte in here. But there are some delicious dishes anyone might enjoy. Mostly you get something much more valuable — recipes that offer sanity and more time outside the kitchen. Plus a few bonuses, such as advice on how to cope when the outside world wants your cooking.

Be forewarned. Canned tomatoes, rice mixes, and frozen vegetables are occasionally used in the recipes. If you tilt your nose up at such things, then you are not a candidate for Seat-of-the-Pants Suppers. Part of the battle of assembling a good meal is knowing which ready-made items will do the trick.

Some of the recipes here might be considered retro; others reflect contemporary tastes. To be included in this book a recipe must take 30 minutes or less to prepare, use a minimum of ingredients, need very little tending, or require just one pot. Simple, satisfying, and fast are the trademarks of a S.O.T.P. Supper.

Thumb through this book with a new attitude about the oft-dreaded dinner chore. Try a few new dishes on your family. Adapt the recipes to your tastes. Cut back on the take-out and make your skillet sizzle. Share Seat-of-the-Pants Suppers with your friends. We need to help each other get through the busy days of our lives deliciously and nutritiously.

# Items to Keep Around

   Even seat-of-the-pants cooking takes some advance work. Here are a few items worth stocking. These keep for a long time, are easy to use and store, and enhance quick home cooking.

- Minced fresh garlic in a jar. This keeps indefinitely in the refrigerator.
- Onions. If you like, you can chop and store these in the freezer in a reclosable plastic bag until ready to use.
- Green peppers. Can be chopped and stored the same way.
- A variety of dried herbs and spices
- A bottle of lemon juice or several lemons for fresh juice
- Shredded cheeses of different kinds
- Bottle of cooking wine and cooking sherry
- Your favorite barbecue sauce
- Pesto. This keeps in the refrigerator a few weeks or freezes well and defrosts quickly
- Soy sauce
- Bread crumbs, plain and seasoned
- Your favorite salsa
- Several cans of diced or crushed tomatoes, tomato paste, and tomato sauce
- Canned legumes (black beans, chick peas, etc.)
- Condensed cream of chicken, celery, or mushroom soup. Choose the lower-salt varieties.
- Chicken and beef stock. Also, instant bouillon for when

5

you run out of canned stock.
- A few packages of ramen noodle soup mixes. These cook quickly and come in handy to expand soups into hearty meals.
- Butter and margarine
- Eggs
- Grains. Rice, couscous, etc.
- Pasta. All shapes and sizes. As much as you can fit in your cabinet.
- Roasting bags, aluminum foil, plastic wrap
- Mainstays: mustard, flour, mayonnaise, salt, pepper, vegetable oils, vinegar, sugar, honey, ketchup, cornstarch

## Other Things You Don't Want to Do Without:

- Refrigerator with ample freezer space
- Microwave oven
- Large skillet and large soup pot for one-dish meals
- Crock pot, also called a slow cooker. (Trust me, you will grow to love this last one.)

## You are primed for efficiency!

*Note: These recipes serve four people, depending on appetites. In some recipes, specific can sizes are not given. A few ounces either way won't matter. Suggestions for side dishes or garnishes are noted at the end of a recipe. The following common abbreviations are used: Tbs. for tablespoon, tsp. for teaspoon, c. for cup, oz. for ounce.*

# No-panic Poultry:
# Chicken and Turkey Dishes

Tips:

- Roast a chicken or a turkey on Sunday, freeze the leftovers, and use in several of the following recipes.

- Use a rotisserie chicken from the deli counter at the supermarket for recipes that call for cut-up chicken.

- Keep boneless, skinless chicken breasts in the freezer. They defrost quickly in the microwave and are a snap to prepare in many different ways. They are lower in fat than other cuts.

- For a change, use ground turkey instead of ground beef in spaghetti sauces and tacos.

# Crusty Lemon Chicken

*This is a mainstay in our household.*

1 lb. boneless chicken breasts, cut in four serving pieces
1 c. Italian seasoned bread crumbs
1/4 c. olive oil
1 Tbs. butter
Juice of one lemon

Dredge individual portions of chicken in bread crumbs. Do not skimp on crumbs. Heat half of olive oil, all of butter, and lemon juice in skillet. Fry dredged chicken over medium heat in skillet until brown and crusty. Turn chicken over. Add rest of olive oil to pan and fry other side of cutlets until cooked through. Remove from heat and garnish with lemon slices and parsley. If desired, add a slice of mozzarella cheese to the top of each portion and let it melt before serving.

# No Fuss Chicken Curry

*Use spices depending on your audience's taste buds.*

1 lb. boneless chicken breasts, sliced in strips
2 Tbs. vegetable oil
1 onion, chopped
1 apple, coarsely chopped
4 ripe tomatoes or one 14-oz. can diced tomatoes, with juice
1/4 c. tomato paste
1/4 c. water
2 Tbs. curry powder
1/2 to 1 tsp. coriander
1/2 to 1 tsp. turmeric
1/2 to 1 tsp. cumin
8 oz. plain yogurt

Saute chicken and onion in vegetable oil in skillet until chicken is no longer pink. Add chopped apple. In medium bowl mix rest of ingredients except yogurt. Add to skillet, cover, and simmer until chicken is done, about 5-10 minutes. Remove from heat. Add salt and pepper if needed. Stir in yogurt to taste. Delicious over basmati rice.

# Chicken with Artichokes

*My husband, who loves marinated artichoke hearts, came up with this delicious meal.*

1 to 1 1/2 lb. boneless chicken breasts
1 can condensed cream of chicken soup
1 c. white wine or cooking sherry
1 8-oz. package presliced mushrooms
1 small jar marinated artichoke hearts, drained and coarsely chopped
1 red pepper, chopped
3 Tbs. butter
1/2 c. seasoned bread crumbs

Grease shallow casserole dish. Place chicken breasts, cut into individual serving pieces, in single layer in dish. Combine soup and wine in bowl. Add mushrooms, artichoke hearts, and red pepper. Pour over chicken. Cover with bread crumbs and dot with butter. Bake 30 minutes uncovered in 325° oven.

# Spanish Chicken over Rice

*The chicken in this dish falls off the bone, the sauce is tasty, and the crock pot does it all. Dump your ingredients in the pot in the morning and leave for the day. When you return, cook your rice. The spiciness of this dish can be adjusted by how much salsa you use (add more if you like) and how hot it is.*

6 to 8 pieces cut up chicken, skin on or off (I like to use skinless, boneless chicken thighs.)
1/2 tsp. garlic powder
Salt and pepper to taste
1 cup beer
1 6-oz. can tomato paste
1/3 c. salsa
3 c. cooked rice

Sprinkle chicken with salt, pepper, and garlic powder. Place in crock pot. Mix beer, tomato paste, and salsa in a bowl. Pour over chicken. Stir once to coat chicken. Cover with lid of crock pot. Cook on low for 8-10 hours or on high 4-6 hours. Remove chicken from sauce, shred it, and return to pot. Serve over rice with a green salad on the side.

# Ah, So Easy Chinese Chicken

1 lb. boneless chicken breast, cut in strips
4 Tbs. vegetable oil
1 tsp. minced garlic
1/2 tsp. powdered ginger or 1 tsp. minced fresh ginger
2-3 scallions, diced, including some of the bright green
tops for garnish
2-4 c. vegetables suitable for stir-fry (shredded cabbage,
carrots, snow peas, sugar snap peas, colored peppers,
broccoli, bok choy, celery, or green beans)
1 small can sliced water chestnuts (optional)
1/3 c. hoisin sauce
1 Tbs. oyster or barbecue sauce
1/2 c. peanuts or cashews, chopped (optional)

Heat 2 Tbs. vegetable oil in wok or skillet until very hot.
Add garlic and ginger and saute 1 minute. Add chicken to
wok and stir-fry 5 minutes or until done. Remove to plate.
Add 2 Tbs. vegetable oil to wok and heat until very hot.
Add vegetables and white part of scallions. Stir-fry over
high heat until vegetables are cooked but still remain
somewhat crisp — about 5 minutes. Add water chestnuts
and stir-fry 1 more minute. Return chicken to wok and
toss with vegetables. Stir hoisin sauce and oyster sauce
into dish. Heat through. Serve over rice with nuts and
green tops of scallions sprinkled on top.

# Creamy Chicken with Lemon and Herbs

1 lb. boneless chicken breasts
1 can condensed cream of chicken soup
Juice of one half lemon (2 Tbs.)
1/2 tsp. each dried basil and thyme
1/4 tsp. pepper

Cut chicken into serving pieces. Place in crock pot. Mix other ingredients in small bowl. Add to crock pot. Stir to coat chicken. Cover and cook on low 8-10 hours. Serve with noodles or mashed potatoes.

**Oven method:**

Preheat oven to 325°. Place chicken breasts in greased, oven-proof dish. Mix other ingredients together and pour over chicken. Sprinkle top with 1/3 c. seasoned bread crumbs if desired. Bake uncovered for about 30 minutes or until done.

# Honey Mustard Chicken

1 lb. boneless chicken breasts, cut into thin strips
2 Tbs. butter or olive oil
1 Tbs. Dijon mustard
1 Tbs. honey
1 c. chicken broth or bouillon
1 tsp. cornstarch
Salt and pepper to taste

Saute chicken strips in oil or butter in large skillet until just cooked through. Mix remaining ingredients in a small bowl. Stir into chicken. Simmer a few minutes until sauce bubbles and thickens and chicken is done. Serve over flat noodles or rice.

15

# Chicken Pumpkin Chowder

*This hearty soup, almost a stew, has everything in it —
protein, vegetable, starch — and pleases young and old.
Kids won't be able to taste the pumpkin, guaranteed. From
Sue Elsaesser.*

1 Tbs. vegetable oil
1/2 lb. boneless chicken breasts, cubed
1 c. onion, chopped
1 red pepper, chopped
1 tsp. minced garlic
1 quart chicken stock
1 16-oz. can solid pack pumpkin
1/2 c. frozen corn kernels or one small can corn, drained
1/2 c. white rice, uncooked
1/2 tsp. dried basil
Salt and pepper to taste

Heat oil in large heavy saucepan over medium heat. Add
chicken, onion, pepper, and garlic. Saute until chicken is no
longer pink. Stir in stock, pumpkin, corn, rice, and spices.
Bring mixture to a boil; cover. Reduce heat and simmer 20
minutes, stirring occasionally, until rice is tender. Serve
with bread and salad for a satisfying meal.

# Chicken in White Wine Sauce

*So simple, it ought to be illegal.*

1 to 1 1/2 lb. boneless chicken pieces, white or dark meat
1 can condensed cream of mushroom soup
1/2 c. white wine
1/2 c. sour cream, lowfat or regular

Place chicken in crock pot. Mix soup, wine, and sour cream. Pour over chicken to coat. Place lid on crock pot and cook on low 7-10 hours. When ready to serve, remove chicken pieces from crock pot, cut or shred into smaller pieces, and return to sauce. Serve over rice or flat noodles.

# Chicken Breasts with Rosemary and Lemon

1 lb. boneless chicken breasts
1/4 c. flour
Salt and pepper to taste
2 Tbs. olive oil
2 Tbs. butter
2 tsp. minced garlic
1 Tbs. dried rosemary or 2 Tbs. chopped fresh rosemary
1/2 c. dry white wine
2 Tbs. fresh lemon juice
2 Tbs. chopped fresh parsley or 1 Tbs. parsley flakes

Cut chicken into serving pieces and flatten. Dredge the
chicken in flour and sprinkle with salt and pepper. Heat
oil and butter in large skillet. Add garlic and saute
briefly. Add chicken and rosemary. Over medium-high heat,
cook chicken uncovered about 4 minutes on each side, until
pieces are nicely browned. Drain fat from skillet. Add
wine, lemon juice, and parsley to skillet. Cover tightly and
simmer 3 minutes, until sauce is slightly thickened.

## Chicken Picante

1 to 1 1/2  lbs. boneless chicken breasts, cut in individual
serving pieces
1 c. picante sauce or taco sauce or salsa
2 Tbs. brown sugar
1 Tbs. prepared mustard
1 c. white rice, uncooked
1 3/4 c. water

Preheat oven to 350°. Grease shallow oven-proof casserole
dish. Spread rice on bottom and around sides of dish. Place
chicken in single layer in dish and on top of some of the
rice. Add water to corners of dish so that rice is
completely covered. Combine picante sauce, brown sugar,
and mustard in a bowl. Pour over chicken. Cover tightly
with aluminum foil. Bake 30-40 minutes or until chicken is
done and rice is tender.

# Chicken Soy Saute

*From Emily Swan: "This is real kid food, but at least it's not chicken nuggets!"*

1 lb. boneless chicken, cut in bite-size pieces
1 clove garlic, pressed, or 1/2 tsp. minced garlic
1 Tbs. soy sauce
1 Tbs. vegetable oil

Toss chicken briefly in a bowl with garlic and soy sauce to coat chicken. Try to do this a little ahead of time, so chicken can absorb the flavors. Heat oil in a skillet and saute chicken pieces until done.

# Asian Chicken Salad

*Make the chicken soy saute from the previous page, serve some to the kids, and use the rest to make this crunchy and delicious salad for the grown-ups.*

About 4 c. of Asian salad greens and/or chopped bok choy, colored peppers, celery, carrots, cabbage, etc.
1 bunch scallions, chopped
2 c. cooked chicken, warm, cold, or room temperature
2 packages ramen noodle soup mix
1/4 c. sesame seeds
3 Tbs. vegetable oil
**Dressing:**
1/4 c. rice or cider vinegar
2 Tbs. soy sauce
1/2 c. salad oil
1/4 c. sugar
1 tsp. sesame oil (optional)

Assemble greens or chopped vegetables and scallions in a large bowl. Top with chicken. In small microwavable bowl combine dressing ingredients. Microwave until mixture bubbles. Let cool slightly while you crumble and brown ramen noodles in vegetable oil in skillet. (Save seasoning packet from mix for another use.) Add sesame seeds to skillet and brown these a bit, too. Combine dressing and noodles in bowl with vegetables and chicken. Serve immediately or wait half an hour to let vegetables wilt a little and absorb flavors.

# Chicken Foil Dinner

*Fancy enough campfire food for the indoor supper table. This cooks while you take your bath. Each diner gets his or her own foil packet. Easy cleanup, too. Who wants to do dishes after a bubble bath?*

4 chicken breasts or thighs
4 squares aluminum foil
Garlic powder
1/4 tsp. thyme
Salt and pepper to taste
4 carrots
4 ribs celery
3-4 potatoes, depending on size
2 Tbs. butter

Place each chicken piece on a large square of aluminum foil. Sprinkle with salt, pepper, garlic, thyme. Slice one carrot and one rib celery for each portion. Add cubed potatoes and a pat of butter. Close foil tightly. Place on cookie sheet or in shallow roasting pan and bake 1 hour at 350°.

# Broiled Chicken Vinaigrette

*Save cooking time by pounding boneless chicken breasts flat, which also helps to tenderize the chicken. This dish marinates for only 5 minutes. It can be grilled instead of broiled.*

4 boneless chicken breasts (about 1 lb.)
3 Tbs. olive oil
3 Tbs. balsamic vinegar
1 tsp. minced garlic
1/2 tsp. salt
1/8 tsp. pepper
Lemon, orange, or kiwi slices for garnish (optional)

Preheat broiler to high or start grill. Mix olive oil, vinegar, garlic, salt, and pepper in a small bowl to make a marinade. Pound individual chicken breasts with a mallet between two pieces of waxed paper until about 1/4-inch thick. Place chicken in shallow glass or ceramic bowl and pour marinade over. Turn chicken to coat with marinade. Let stand 5 minutes. Line broiling or roasting pan with aluminum foil for easy cleanup. Place chicken in single layer on foil. Broil about 6 inches from heat for 5 minutes. Turn chicken, baste with pan drippings, and broil another 4-7 minutes or until chicken is no longer pink inside. Garnish with fruit slices or parsley and serve.

# Moroccan Chicken

*A one-pot meal with an unusual flavor.*

1 lb. boneless chicken breasts, cubed
1 Tbs. olive oil
1 onion, chopped
2 tsp. minced garlic
1 Tbs. vegetable oil
1 red pepper, chopped
2-3 carrots, sliced
1 zucchini, diced
1 quart chicken broth
1 Tbs. paprika
2 tsp. cumin
1/2 tsp. coriander
1/2 tsp. cinnamon
1/4 tsp. cayenne pepper
1 c. white rice, uncooked

Saute onions, garlic, and chicken in oil in a large saucepan until chicken is no longer pink. Add everything else. Bring to boil. Reduce heat and simmer uncovered, stirring occasionally, about 20 minutes or until rice is tender.

# Chicken Ragout with No Goo Cleanup

*Return home to assemble this dinner made in a roasting bag and using whatever vegetables you have in the produce drawer. Or mix everything ahead and refrigerate in the bag. Be sure to cut longer-cooking root vegetables, such as potatoes, into small pieces to cook thoroughly.*

6 skinless boneless chicken thighs
1 large oven roasting bag
1 14-oz. can diced tomatoes with juice, or pureed tomatoes
1 tsp. minced garlic
1 onion, chopped coarsely
2-3 ribs celery, thinly sliced
2-3 carrots, thinly sliced
2 c. potatoes, finely cubed, or other vegetables such as zucchini, broccoli, cauliflower
1 tsp. thyme
1 tsp. basil
1 Tbs. flour

Preheat oven to 350°. Put chicken in roasting bag. Mix everything else in a bowl and pour over and around chicken. Close bag with tie and cut 3 tiny slits in top. Place bag in roasting pan and bake for 40 minutes. Cut bag open, carefully dump contents in clean bowl, and serve with bread on the side. Say hello to your entire meal.

# Kid-Friendly Chicken Casserole

*This casserole is khaki-colored, but that contributes to its homey charm, according to Debbie Johnson whose kids can't get enough of it. She insists that this be made with Franco-American Chicken Gravy from a can. So noted. Make extra rice some night to have on hand in the refrigerator along with the leftover chicken.*

2-3 c. cooked cut-up chicken
1 can chicken gravy
3 c. cooked rice (use 5-minute rice, if necessary)
3 Tbs. butter
1 c. seasoned bread crumbs

Grease bottom of shallow casserole dish. Mix chicken, rice, and gravy and place in dish. Melt butter in microwavable bowl or on stovetop, add bread crumbs, and mix. Top casserole with crumb mixture. Bake 20 minutes at 350° or until very hot.

# Indian Chicken

1 c. plain yogurt
2 tsp. minced garlic
1 Tbs. curry powder
1 Tbs. paprika
1/2 tsp. salt
1 to 1 1/2 lbs. boneless chicken breasts, cut in serving pieces and pounded flat
3 cups cooked rice

Put rice up to boil. Preheat broiler. Combine yogurt and seasonings in large bowl. Add chicken to yogurt mixture and let sit a few minutes. Line broiling pan with aluminum foil. Place chicken in single layer on foil. Top with excess yogurt mixture. Broil 5 minutes, until browned. Turn, baste with yogurt sauce again, and broil other side until cooked through, about 5-8 minutes depending on thickness. Garnish with parsley, scallions, or fresh cilantro and serve with rice.

# Easy Enchiladas

*A great use of leftover poultry, from Sue Elsaesser.
"Much greater than the sum of its parts." —Jeff*

1 onion, chopped
2 Tbs. vegetable oil
1 1/2 c. cooked chicken or turkey, shredded or cubed
1 12-oz. jar picante sauce
3 oz. cream cheese (or use sour cream, in a pinch)
1 tsp. cumin
2 c. cheddar cheese, shredded
8 6-inch flour tortillas

Heat oven to 350°. Cook onion in oil in large skillet until tender. Stir in chicken, 1/4 cup picante sauce, cream cheese, and cumin. Heat through. Stir in 1 cup cheese. Spoon about 1/4 cup of this mixture in center of each tortilla and roll up. Place seam-side down in large rectangular oven-proof dish. Top with rest of picante sauce and cheese. Bake 15 minutes.

# Chicken or Turkey Tetrazzini

*Another use for Sunday leftovers. This recipe skips the traditional part where the tetrazzini goes in the oven to get crisp on top. Instead it's a quicker and creamier dish served right out of the skillet and sprinkled with cheese.*

12 oz. linguine or pasta of your choice
2 c. fresh or frozen cut-up vegetables such as broccoli, carrots, celery, and/or cauliflower (optional)
2 Tbs. butter or olive oil
1 onion, chopped
1 green pepper, chopped
1 tsp. minced garlic
2 Tbs. flour
2-3 c. cooked chicken or turkey, cutup
1 c. chicken stock
2 Tbs. sherry
2/3 c. whole milk or cream
1 tsp. basil
1 tsp. thyme
1/4 tsp. pepper
1 c. grated parmesan cheese

Cook pasta and drain. Add optional vegetables to water to cook along with the pasta. Meanwhile, saute onion, pepper, and garlic in butter in skillet until tender. Stir in flour and stock and cook until thickened. Mix in chicken, milk, herbs, sherry, and pepper. Stir and heat to a scald. Add pasta, toss mixture, top with cheese, and serve.

# Spicy Chicken Stew

*This serves eight, so cut it in half for four people. Or make it all and enjoy the leftovers. A contribution from Sue Elsaesser.*

2 lbs. boneless chicken breasts, cut into strips
3 c. salsa
4 Tbs. vegetable oil
1 onion, chopped
4 tsp. minced garlic
2 quarts chicken stock
1 c. dry white wine
5 carrots, sliced
4 potatoes, cubed
1/4 tsp. salt
2 c. tricolor rotini pasta
Sour cream for topping (optional)

Heat oil in large deep pot over medium heat. Saute onion and garlic. Add chicken and saute it until no longer pink. Add everything but pasta and salsa to pot, cover, and simmer 10 minutes. When vegetables are tender, add salsa and rotini. Cook uncovered 10 more minutes. Ladle into bowls and top with a spoonful of sour cream. Garnish with cilantro.

# Turkey Sloppy Joes

1 lb. ground turkey
1 Tbs. vegetable oil
1 onion, chopped
1 tsp. cumin
1 tsp. oregano
3/4 c. Heinz chili sauce
1 6-oz. can tomato paste
1 c. water
4-6 bulky rolls, split

Heat oil in skillet. Brown turkey in oil with chopped onion until turkey is cooked through. Drain fat. Stir in all other ingredients and simmer a few minutes to meld flavors and until desired consistency. Serve over split bulky rolls.

# Salsa Chicken on the Run

*An easy microwave recipe from Charlotte Agell. This is good with rice or noodles.*

1 lb. boneless chicken breasts
1/3 to 1 c. or more of your favorite salsa (Charlotte uses a peach salsa.)
1/2 to 1 c. cheddar cheese (optional)

Cut the chicken breasts into serving pieces. Place in single layer in microwavable dish with sides. Pour salsa over chicken. (The amount usually depends on what you have left over and sitting in the frig.) Cover with microwavable plastic wrap, vent it slightly, and microwave dish for 5-10 minutes, depending on your microwave's power, until chicken is cooked throughout. Turn dish once during cooking. Carefully remove plastic wrap. Spoon any salsa drippings on top of chicken. Sprinkle with cheese (or not) and place dish under broiler to melt the cheese or crisp up a the top a bit.

# Meaty Stuff

Tips:

- Slow cookers, or crock pots, tenderize tougher cuts of meat. Even better, they use low, slow heat so they can be left on while you're out of the house. Follow the directions that come with your slow cooker when trying the recipes in this book. With a tiny bit of preparation in the morning, you can come home to a hearty meal and a savory aroma in the kitchen, which is especially nice in the fall and winter.

- Ground beef must be cooked until no pink remains, but this is not true of other cuts of beef; do not overcook them.

- A pound of hamburger in the freezer offers a sense of culinary security for some people. Choose a variety with a low fat content. You can partially defrost the beef in the microwave and then brown it in a skillet to use in myriad ways, such as in Half-hour Chili. Or make a quick spaghetti sauce with it, using sauteed onions and peppers, a jar or two of your favorite spaghetti sauce or canned tomatoes, tomato paste, spices, and a squirt of wine. Most likely you'll have enough leftover sauce to freeze for another meal.

# Quick Beef Stroganoff with Sour Pickle

1 lb. fairly tender cut of beef, such as top round
Salt and pepper to taste
1/4 tsp. paprika
1/4 tsp. garlic powder
2 Tbs. butter or oil
1/2 c. sliced onion
1 c. red wine or cooking sherry
1 c. sour cream
1 large sour pickle, sliced into thin, one-inch strips
12 oz. flat noodles

Cut beef into thin strips. Season with salt, pepper, paprika, and garlic powder. Heat butter or oil in skillet. Saute meat 3 minutes, or until brown on outside. Do not overcook. Remove from skillet. Saute onion in skillet, adding more butter or oil if necessary. Add wine, simmer until reduced almost by half, return meat to skillet. Simmer 1 minute more and add sour pickle. Mix in sour cream and warm dish through. Serve over cooked noodles.

# Beanless Chili in a Crock Pot

*The name says it all. Very easy.*

1 lb. stew beef, cut in cubes
2 c. chopped onion
1 Tbs. minced garlic
1 tsp. oregano
1 tsp. cumin
2 Tbs. chili powder (more or less to taste)
1 14-oz. can diced tomatoes with juice
1/4 c. beef broth or bouillon

Combine all ingredients in crock pot and cook on low 8 to 10 hours.

# Miami Beef

*The entire meal in a skillet. This is also nice with rolls and a salad and sliced oranges on the side.*

1 lb. top round of beef, cut in thin strips
4 Tbs. vegetable oil
1 onion, sliced
2 green or red peppers, or 1 of each, chopped coarsely
2 large potatoes, washed and cut in half-inch cubes
1 14-oz. can diced tomatoes, drained
3 Tbs. soy sauce
2 Tbs. balsamic vinegar
1/4 tsp. cumin
Salt and pepper to taste

Heat 2 Tbs. of oil in a large skillet or wok and sear beef over high heat until brown on the outside. Remove to a plate. Add rest of oil to skillet and fry onions, peppers, and potatoes over medium-high heat, stirring occasionally, until potatoes are done, about 10-12 minutes. Add rest of ingredients. Return beef to skillet and toss. Simmer, covered, 2-3 minutes, or until beef is just done.

# Cheating Jambalaya

*Lynn Heinz's method is so simple it had to be included.*

1 box Zatarain's jambalaya rice mix (found in gourmet section of many supermarkets)
2-3 cups Hilshire Farm turkey kielbasa, cut in diagonal slices
Vegetable oil
1 can beer
1-2 c. chopped raw vegetables, such as celery, peppers, carrots, squash, parsley, etc. (optional)

Brown kielbasa slices in very little oil in large saucepan. Add Jambalaya rice mix and liquid according to package directions, using 1/2 beer and 1/2 water for the required liquid. Add optional vegetables to pot before simmering. Cover and simmer until rice is done, about 25 minutes.

# Roast Beef Crostini

1 large loaf French or Italian bread
1 Tbs. olive oil
1/2 tsp. garlic powder
1 lb. sliced deli roast beef
1/2 red onion, thinly sliced
1 bell pepper, thinly sliced
1-2 c. shredded or grated cheese — a mixture of
mozzarella and parmesan is good

Slice loaf of bread lengthwise. Brush with olive oil and
sprinkle with garlic powder. Layer with roast beef, then
thin slices of onion and pepper. Spread cheese on top.
Bake open faced at 450° for 6-8 minutes, until bread is
toasted and cheese is bubbly. Cool slightly and cut in
serving pieces.

# One-skillet Supper

*Your basic American chop suey in a skillet.*

1 Tbs. olive oil
1 tsp. minced garlic
1 onion, chopped
1 lb. ground beef or turkey
1 14-oz. can low-salt beef stock
1 14-oz. can Italian-style diced tomatoes, with juice
2 1/2 c. uncooked pasta, such as rotini or elbows
2 Tbs. tomato paste (optional)
1 c. cheddar or mozzarella cheese, grated

In a large skillet saute garlic and onion in olive oil briefly. Add ground beef or turkey and brown. Drain fat. Add stock, tomatoes with juice, and pasta. Add a little water (1/4 to 1/2 c.) if necessary to just cover the pasta. Bring to boil. Cook uncovered until pasta is done and liquid is mostly gone (about 15 minutes). Stir in tomato paste. Sprinkle top with cheese. Turn off heat. Wait a minute until cheese melts. Serve.

# Sweet and Sour Beef

*Use any kind of ground meat for this: beef, lamb, venison, moose . . . .*

1 to 1 1/2 lb. ground beef or other ground meat
1 Tbs. vegetable oil
1/2 onion, chopped
1/4 c. molasses
1/4 c. vinegar
3/4 c. ketchup
3 c. cooked rice

Saute onion in oil briefly. Add meat and cook until completely brown. Drain fat. Combine rest of ingredients except rice in a small bowl. Add to meat. Simmer a couple of minutes, adding a few tablespoons of water if necessary to maintain a sauce. Serve over hot rice.

# Half-hour (or Less) Chili

*From Sue Elsaesser. Good with cornbread — or not!*

1 lb. ground beef
1 tsp. minced garlic
2 16-oz. jars chunky picante sauce
1 can pinto beans, drained and rinsed
1 Tbs. fresh cilantro (optional)
1/2 c. cheddar cheese (optional)

Brown garlic and beef in skillet. Add picante sauce and beans. Simmer 30 minutes or until you are too hungry to wait any longer. Top with chopped cilantro and/or cheddar cheese if desired. Done.

# Corn Bread

*If you are so inclined, bake this while Half-hour Chili simmers. Otherwise, put up some rice and your feet.*

1 1/4 c. flour
3/4 c. cornmeal
2 Tbs. sugar
2 tsp. baking powder
1/2 tsp. salt
1 c. milk
1/4 c. oil
1 egg, beaten

Heat oven to 400°. Grease 8- or 9-inch square pan. Combine first five ingredients in large bowl. Stir in milk, oil, and egg until just blended. Pour in pan. Bake 20-25 minutes, until bread is golden brown on top and toothpick poked in center comes out clean. After it cools slightly, cut cornbread into large squares, split in half lengthwise, and spoon chili over top. Or serve on the side with butter.

# Beef Stroganoff, Sort of

*This is an easy pleaser in our house.*

1 1/2 lb. stew beef, cubed
1 envelop onion soup mix
1 can cream of mushroom soup
1/2 c. red wine
12 oz. cooked flat noodles

Combine all ingredients in a crock pot. Cover and cook on low 8-10 hours. Serve over hot noodles.

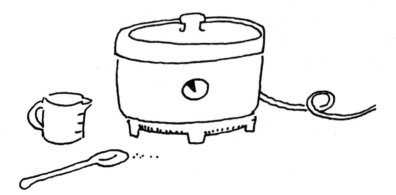

# Barbecued Pork

*Jean Doughty, who works as a teacher, told me about this simple, family-pleasing crock pot meal. If you took the number of soccer fields her teenage girls have played on and laid them end to end, you'd probably get to the moon and back. Jean gets to most games, so that means dinner has to be easy and quick. Check out her creative combo — tortillas and pulled pork. Well, why not?*

1 lb. pork tenderloin or boneless chicken breasts
1 bottle of your favorite barbecue sauce
6 bulky rolls or 8 flour tortillas
1-2 tomatoes, chopped (optional)
Shredded lettuce (optional)

Cut meat to fit and place in crock pot. Dump entire bottle of barbecue sauce over all. Cover crock pot. Cook on low 8-10 hours. When done, cool meat slightly and shred it into sauce. To serve, spoon mixture over split bulky rolls. Or place barbecued pork or chicken in center of a warmed tortilla, add tomatoes and shredded lettuce, roll up, and eat.

This is great with **Cole Slaw**: Buy cole slaw mix in bag in produce section (usually 16 oz., or about 4 c.). Stir in 1 tsp. salt, 1/2 tsp. pepper, 1/3 c. mayonnaise, and 2 Tbs. lemon juice or vinegar.

# La-de-dah Lamb Stew

*You can also use beef or veal for this crock pot dish. It makes a nice sauce to go over rice or noodles.*

1 1/2 lbs. lamb stew meat, in cubes
1/4 c. chili sauce
1/4 c. apricot jam
1 envelope onion soup mix

Place meat in crock pot. Mix rest of ingredients together in small bowl. Pour over meat, then stir to coat. Place lid on crock pot and cook 8-10 hours on low.

## Pork Chops with Lemon and Thyme

4 pork chops, about half-inch thick
Salt and pepper to taste
2 Tbs. flour
1 Tbs. butter or vegetable oil
1 tsp. garlic
2 tsp. thyme
2 Tbs. lemon juice
1/2 c. chicken bouillon

Sprinkle pork chops with salt and pepper and rub with flour. Melt butter in skillet and saute garlic for 2 minutes. Add pork chops to skillet in single layer and brown about 3 minutes each side over medium heat. Add everything else. Cover skillet, lower heat, and simmer 10-15 minutes or until pork is done (when no pink remains).

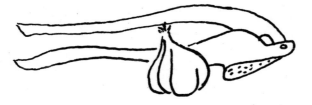

# Pork Chops with Orange Sauce and Orzo

4 pork chops, about half-inch thick
Salt and pepper to taste
2 Tbs. flour
1 Tbs. butter or vegetable oil
1 tsp. garlic
1/2 c. orange juice
1 Tbs. molasses
2-3 c. cooked orzo

Sprinkle pork chops with salt and pepper and rub with flour. Melt butter in skillet and saute garlic for 2 minutes. Add pork chops to skillet in single layer and brown about 3 minutes each side over medium heat. Mix molasses and orange juice and add to skillet. Simmer, covered, about 10-15 minutes or until pork is done (when no pink remains). Garnish with orange slices and parsley and serve with orzo, rice, or noodles.

# Pasta Possibilities

Tips:

- Low fat and easy to prepare, pasta can be the foundation of a hearty supper or a cool main dish salad.

- When boiling pasta, add a little oil to the pot (a scant tablespoon) to keep it from sticking together when drained.

- Keep lots of nonperishable pasta in the pantry, in all shapes and sizes. Each shape has its own versatility: angel hair cooks in two minutes, rotini holds sauces well. All are quick to prepare.

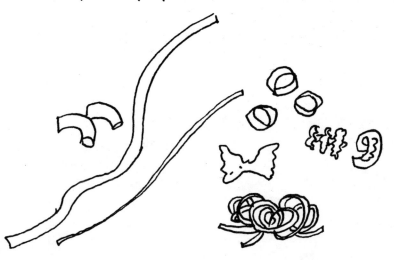

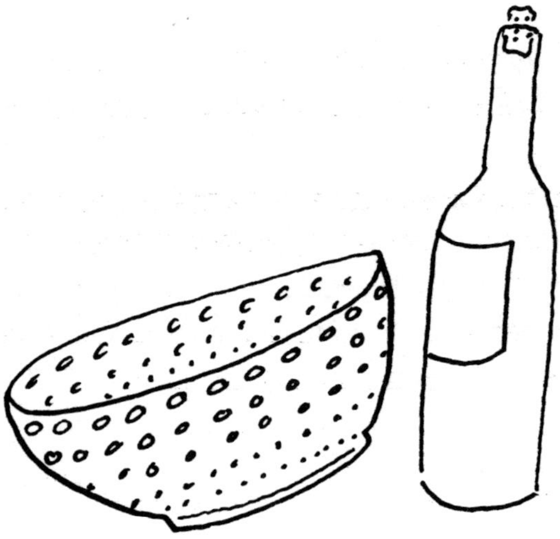

# Pesto and Feta Pasta

*Sherry Hanson, master of efficiency, e-mailed this recipe to me within seconds of hearing about this book. The dish is now very popular in my house.*

1 16-oz. box penne pasta
1 small container of pesto, about 7 oz.
8 oz. crumbled feta cheese
1/2 c. sun-dried tomatoes, cut into pieces with scissors

Cook pasta and drain. Toss with all other ingredients and serve. This is very nice with a salad.

# Linguine with Clam Sauce

*The beauty of this dish is that nothing comes from the refrigerator, so you can keep everything it requires on hand for weeks or months. The dish takes 15 minutes to prepare and is very satisfying.*

1 16-oz. box linguine or spaghetti
2 Tbs. olive oil
1 tsp. minced garlic
2 6-oz. cans minced clams, drained
1/3 c. white wine (Use half of one of those single serving bottles and sip the other half.)
1 Tbs. basil
1 Tbs. lemon juice
1 28-oz. can crushed tomatoes
1 tsp. sugar
Parmesan cheese for topping

Saute garlic in olive oil briefly in large skillet. Add everything but minced clams and linguine to skillet. Simmer 10 minutes, stirring occasionally. Meanwhile, cook linguine in large pot of boiling water, drain. Add clams to skillet. Simmer 2 more minutes. Serve clam sauce over linguine topped with lots of grated parmesan cheese.

# Penne with Tomato Cream Sauce

*The sauce cooks as fast as the pasta.*

1 lb. penne pasta
2 Tbs. olive oil
1 Tbs. minced garlic
1/2 onion, thinly sliced or diced
1 28-oz. can crushed tomatoes with puree
1/4 tsp. cayenne pepper
2 tsp. dried basil or 2 Tbs. chopped fresh basil
1 c. light or heavy cream or whole milk
Parmesan cheese for topping

Boil water and cook pasta while you make the sauce as
follows: Saute onions and garlic in oil in large saucepan
for 3 minutes. Add tomatoes, cayenne, and basil to pan and
simmer over medium heat 5 minutes. Turn heat to medium
low and stir in cream. Heat sauce to a scald, immediately
remove from heat, and serve over drained pasta topped
with grated parmesan cheese.

# Angel Hair Pasta with Bacon and Peppers

*Put together a delicious meal using a minimum of ingredients and quick-cooking angel hair pasta.*

1 tsp. minced garlic
1 onion, chopped
2 Tbs. olive oil
3 peppers, chopped (mixing colors is nice)
6 strips bacon, chopped
1 14-oz. can diced tomatoes, slightly drained (optional)
12 oz. angel hair pasta, or pasta of your choice, cooked and drained
2 Tbs. melted butter
1 c. grated parmesan or romano cheese

Saute garlic and onion in oil in skillet until onion is translucent. Add peppers and bacon and saute until bacon is brown but not crisp. Do not let the peppers get mushy. If desired add tomatoes to skillet and heat through. Toss cooked pasta with melted butter and then skillet mixture. Sprinkle liberally with grated cheese, and you are ready to sit down and eat.

# Elbows With Creamy Pea Sauce

*This dish, only 15 minutes to table, is nice with a crusty bread.*

1 lb. elbow pasta
1 Tbs. butter or olive oil
1 onion, chopped
1 tsp. minced garlic
1 red or green pepper (red makes a nice contrast)
2 c. light cream
1 10-oz. package frozen peas, thawed
1-2 c. parmesan or romano cheese, shredded
Salt and pepper to taste

Cook elbows in boiling water. Meanwhile, saute onion, garlic, and pepper in butter or olive oil in large saucepan or skillet. Add cream, salt, and black pepper. Scald but do not boil. Stir in thawed peas; heat through. Drain cooked pasta, return to pot, and add cream sauce. Remove from heat, immediately toss with cheese, and serve with another grinding of black pepper if desired.

# What's in the Pantry Pasta

*Who needs those expensive mixes?*

1 lb. rotini or any other pasta
1/2 c. olive oil
1 Tbs. each parsley, basil, oregano
1 Tbs. diced onion, or onion flakes in a pinch
1 tsp. minced garlic
2 or 3 c. chopped vegetables, such as carrots, celery,
broccoli, peppers, zucchini, frozen peas (optional)
1 c. shredded parmesan, pecorino, or romano cheese

Cook pasta in boiling water until done. Add optional
chopped vegetables to pasta water for the last few
minutes, to cook along with the pasta; it's perfectly fine
to do without them. Meanwhile, soak herbs, onion, and
garlic in olive oil. Drain pasta, return to pot, toss with
olive oil mixture and any additions. Add cheese and toss
again. Serve.

**Last minute additions:** Chopped marinated artichoke
hearts, chopped roasted red peppers, or a can of well-
drained tuna fish or anchovies. Whatever is in the pantry
and strikes your fancy.

# Linguine with Turkey and Portobello Mushrooms

*This is a yummy inspiration from my sister-in-law, Wendy Amsterdam.*

1 16-oz. box linguine
1/2 to 1 lb. ground turkey
1 portobello mushroom, chopped (or use already sliced mushrooms from the supermarket)
2 Tbs. olive oil
1 onion, chopped
1 tsp. garlic, minced
1 14-oz. can crushed tomatoes
1 tsp. dried basil or 1-2 Tbs. chopped fresh basil
2 Tbs. balsamic vinegar or leftover red wine
Salt and pepper to taste

Boil and drain linguine. Saute onion, garlic, and mushroom in olive oil for 3 minutes. Add turkey and saute until brown. Drain fat. Add tomatoes. Add basil and vinegar or red wine. Add salt and/or pepper to taste. Simmer a few minutes. Serve over linguine.

# Broccoli and Garlic Pasta

*This page and the next — two pasta recipes that are simplicity at its healthy best, from Emily Swan. You can add pine nuts to this one for texture and protein.*

12 oz. rotini or some other easy-to-eat pasta
3-4 c. coarsely chopped broccoli
3 cloves garlic, pressed, or 2 tsp. minced garlic
3 Tbs. olive oil
2 tsp. dried basil or 2 Tbs. chopped fresh basil
1/2 tsp. salt
1/4 tsp. pepper
1/4 c. pine nuts or chopped walnuts (optional)
Parmesan or romano cheese for topping

Cut up and steam broccoli, then refresh under cold water. Boil pasta. Meanwhile, heat olive oil in a skillet. Saute garlic briefly. Add broccoli, basil, salt, pepper, and pine nuts. Saute 3-4 minutes. Drain cooked pasta and toss with broccoli mixture. Serve topped with parmesan or romano cheese.

# Tomato and Garlic Pasta

12 oz. pasta of your choice
6 fresh tomatoes
2 cloves garlic, pressed, or 1 tsp. minced garlic
1/2 c. chopped fresh basil
1/2 tsp. salt
1 c. parmesan cheese

Boil pasta in a large pot. Coarsely chop tomatoes and combine in a bowl with garlic, basil, and salt. You can microwave the mixture for 1-2 minutes to warm and wilt the vegetables, but it is not necessary. Drain cooked pasta and toss it with the tomato mixture. Top with parmesan cheese. Add a good shake or grinding of black pepper if desired. Serve.

# Bernie's Favorite Pasta

*Adult fare, unless the kids really like artichokes and sharp cheese. "This is quick and flexible. You can use your favorite vegetables. I substitute asparagus for broccoli when in season. I've also done this with summer squash and spinach. You can also sub fresh parmesan or romano for the feta cheese." —Bernie Monegain*

12 oz. spaghetti or bow tie pasta
1 bunch broccoli
1/2 lb. sliced mushrooms
2-3 perfect tomatoes, chopped coarsely
1 jar marinated artichoke hearts, drained and chopped
2 Tbs. olive oil
1/4 tsp. pepper
8 oz. crumbled feta cheese

Boil pasta. Chop and steam broccoli and mushrooms until broccoli is bright and still crisp. In a large pot or skillet saute the tomatoes and artichoke hearts in the olive oil for 1 minute. Add cooked pasta and veggies and stir. Sprinkle with feta or another sharp cheese of your choice. Add some freshly ground pepper. Toss and serve.

# Rigatoni With Roasted Vegetables

*You need only an oven roasting pan to make this pasta topping.*

1 lb. rigatoni
1/4 c. olive oil
1/2 onion, chopped
2 tsp. minced garlic
4 cups, more or less, coarsely chopped vegetables for roasting — broccoli, cauliflower, carrots, peppers, winter squash. Use a mixture or just one or two of these.
Salt and pepper to taste
1/4 c. pesto
1/2 to 1 c. parmesan cheese

Preheat oven to 400°. Pour olive oil in roasting pan. Stir in garlic and onion and place pan in oven for 3 minutes to cook them slightly. Remove. Add rest of vegetables to pan. Sprinkle with salt and pepper. Toss to coat with olive oil in pan. Roast uncovered in oven about 25-30 minutes, stirring two or three times. During the last 15 minutes of roasting, boil the rigatoni. Drain. When vegetables are tender and somewhat carmelized, remove pan from oven. Add rigatoni and pesto to vegetables and toss. Serve individual portions topped with a generous sprinkling of parmesan cheese.

# Take-along Casserole

*A portable kid-friendly dish that appears on many a community potluck table. Make it with or without meat. This easily serves 6.*

1 lb. pasta shells, cooked and drained
1/2 to 1 lb. ground beef, browned and drained of fat
1 c. cottage cheese
1 c. sour cream
1 Tbs. Italian seasonings
1/8 tsp. pepper
2 Tbs. parmesan cheese
1 26-oz. jar of your favorite spaghetti sauce
1 c. mozzarella cheese, shredded

Preheat oven to 375°. Combine cottage cheese, sour cream, parmesan cheese, and seasonings in large bowl. Add rest of ingredients except mozzarella cheese and 1 c. of sphaghetti sauce. Spread mixture evenly in large, shallow casserole dish (greased). Dot with rest of sphaghetti sauce and sprinkle with mozzarella cheese. Bake covered for 25 minutes, then 5 minutes uncovered, to melt cheese on top.

# Fancy Ramen Noodles

*Emily Swan's quickest dinner imaginable.*

2 packages of ramen noodle soup mix, cooked according to directions on package or increasing water slightly ("to mitigate the saltiness of the soup" —Emily).
1-3 Tbs. chopped fresh herbs (cilantro is great, chives too)
1-2 c. finely chopped green things (spinach, cabbage, or any other greens, scallions, etc.)

While the ramen noodles are cooking, chop/shred all the green things and herbs and distribute them among the soup bowls. Pour the hot soup directly over the greens, wilting them somewhat, and eat!

Serve grilled cheese sandwiches on the side, or sliced apples with a dip of peanut butter.

# Melissa's Famous Kielbasa Pasta

*Whoever said a smoky meat doesn't belong over pasta has not tried this supper dish which Melissa Pizzolato feeds her family regularly with great success.*

1 Tbs. olive oil
1/2 c. chopped green or red pepper
1 onion, chopped
2 c. sliced or coarsely chopped kielbasa (use lower fat turkey kielbasa if desired)
4-5 chopped fresh tomatoes, or 1 large can tomato puree or plum tomatoes if you are without
Generous shakes of Italian seasonings (oregano, basil, and parsley)
16 oz. linguine or spaghetti

Saute peppers and onions in olive oil until tender. Add kielbasa and brown it over medium heat for a few minutes. Stir in tomatoes or tomato sauce, seasonings, and simmer 5 minutes. Serve over cooked linguine or spaghetti.

# Some Things Fishy:
# Fish and Seafood Suppers

Tips:

- Fish is often overlooked as a simple and quick-cooking supper option. Use cheese, bread crumbs, simple sauces, or marinades to dress it it up.

- Quick, basic techniques for cooking fish include baking, broiling, microwaving, grilling, and pan frying. Very thin fish does not have to be turned when broiled.

- Fish should be as fresh as possible. For best quality, use it the same day you buy it or freeze it immediately. Ask your fishmonger about the freshness of what's on display.

- Fillet of flounder and fillet of sole are essentially the same thing — thin, white, mild-tasting fish without bones.

- Portion sizes can range from 3 to 8 ounces per adult serving, so use your judgement when preparing the following recipes.

## Spicy Fish

*This is nice with rice.*

1 to 1 1/2 lbs. haddock or sole fillets
1 c. salsa
1/2 c. sour cream

Mix salsa and sour cream. Arrange fish in greased baking dish, doubling up or tucking under the ends of very thin pieces to make fish a uniform thickness. Top and surround with salsa mixture. Bake 20 minutes at 350° or until fish is tender.

# Broiled Hawaiian Fish

1 to 1 1/2 lbs. fillet of sole
2 T. vegetable oil
1/3 c. soy sauce
1/2 tsp. powdered ginger or 1 tsp. minced fresh ginger
1 Tbs. brown sugar
1 Tbs. vinegar
1 tsp. minced garlic

Preheat broiler. Place fish fillets in a single layer in a shallow oven-proof dish. You can line dish with aluminum foil for easier clean up if you like. Brush fish with a little vegetable oil to keep it from drying out. Mix rest of ingredients in a bowl. Pour over fillets. Broil about 3-4 inches from heat for 3-8 minutes, depending on thickness of fish, or until fish is just opaque throughout. Do not turn. Spoon sauce over fish and serve garnished with chopped scallion tops or parsley sprigs.

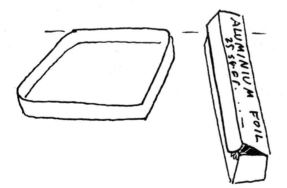

# Emily Swan's Easy Fish Fillets

1 to 1 1/2 lbs. flounder fillets or other thin white fish
Juice of 1/2 lemon (about 2 Tbs.)
Salt and pepper to taste
1/4 c. unseasoned or seasoned bread crumbs
1/4 c. finely grated cheddar or parmesan cheese
3 Tbs. butter

Preheat broiler. Clean and dry fillets and arrange them in
on a foil-covered broiler pan. Sprinkle with lemon juice,
salt, and pepper. Mix cheese and bread crumbs together
and spread over the fish fillets. Dot with butter. Broil
until fish is done, or opaque throughout, about 3-8
minutes depending on thickness. Decorate with lemon
slices.

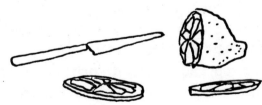

# Fish Plaki

*A Greek way of preparing fish, using the catch of the day. Just pile the ingredients on the fish and bake 20 minutes.*

1 and 1/2 lbs. cod, haddock, halibut, flounder, or sole fillets
1/4 c. olive oil
2 lemons
Salt and pepper to taste
2 tsp. oregano
2 tsp. minced garlic
3 fresh tomatoes, sliced
1 c. fresh parsley, chopped
3 scallions, chopped white part, reserving green stalks
1 c. seasoned or plain bread crumbs
1/4 c. water
2 Tbs. butter

Preheat oven to 350°. Place fish in greased baking dish. Double up slices of very thin fish. Drizzle fish with olive oil and juice of one lemon. Sprinkle with salt, pepper, and oregano. Spread garlic over fish. Place tomato slices, parsley, and scallions on top, and cover with bread crumbs. Dot with butter. Decorate dish with scallion stalks and second lemon, sliced. Add water to corner of dish. Bake uncovered for 20-25 minutes or until fish is tender.

# Baked Sole with Parmesan

1 1/2 lbs. sole fillets
4 Tbs. butter, melted
2 tsp. minced garlic
3 Tbs. grated parmesan cheese
1 fresh tomato, sliced
2 tsp. dried basil or 2 Tbs. chopped fresh basil
Pepper to taste

Preheat oven to 350°. Place fish in greased baking dish in shallow layer (you can double up the fish). Top with thin slices of tomato. Add garlic and basil and a dash of pepper to melted butter. Pour over fish. Top with grated parmesan cheese. Bake 20 minutes or until done.

# Lemon Pepper Fish Baked in Foil

*My cousin, Amy Bach, steams fish in parchment on the stove in a large, tightly covered pot, often including broccoli or another vegetable in the steamer. She is an attorney and was pregnant with her second child when she devised this method of one-pot, no clean-up cooking. The following method uses aluminum foil and the oven. Use pepper according to your palate.*

1 1/2 lbs. sole or haddock fillets
4 squares of aluminum foil
Juice of one lemon (about 4 Tbs.)
3 Tbs. butter, melted
1/4 to 1 tsp. black pepper, or pepper blend
1 tsp. thyme, basil, or rosemary

Preheat oven to 350°. Place individual serving of fish in foil, overlapping thinner fish if necessary. Sprinkle lightly with salt. Mix everything else in a small bowl. Drizzle equally over each fish portion. Close foil tightly. Place in a shallow oven-proof pan with edges. Bake 15 minutes or until fish is done. Serve with rice or couscous.

# Fish Tacos

*A quick and healthy version of tacos that is easily prepared in the microwave oven.*

1 lb. haddock, sole, or flounder fillets
1 c. salsa — the hotter the better
1 onion, chopped
1 green pepper, chopped
1 tsp. minced garlic
1/2 to 1 4-oz. can chopped green chilis, drained (optional)
8 crispy taco shells, heated slightly in oven or microwave

**On side:** sharp cheddar cheese, sour cream, shredded cabbage or lettuce, chopped tomatoes, additional salsa

In microwave-safe bowl, combine fish, onion, garlic, green pepper, optional chilis, and salsa. Cover with plastic wrap, vent slightly, and microwave until fish is done, turning bowl once or twice and cooking 5-12 minutes total, depending on your microwave's power and thickness of fish. (Or you can cook these together in a skillet in a little vegetable oil.) Wait a minute for steam to escape, then carefully remove plastic wrap. Flake fish so it is well mixed in salsa sauce. Drain mixture somewhat. Mound into heated taco shells. Top with cheese, tomatoes, cabbage, sour cream, etc.

# Greek Shrimp

*Simpy broil the shrimp and serve over orzo, rice, or couscous with a no-cook lemon sauce.*

1 1/2 lbs. large shrimp, peeled, tails on or off (they can be broiled either way)
1 Tbs. olive oil
1 tsp. minced garlic
2 Tbs. melted butter
Juice of one lemon (about 4 Tbs.)
1/3 c. olive oil
2 tsp. dill
2 tsp. parsley flakes or 2 Tbs. fresh parsley, chopped
1/2 tsp. salt

Preheat broiler to 550°. Rinse shrimp and pat dry. Line broiler pan with aluminum foil and place shrimp on foil in a single layer. Coat shrimp with olive oil and spread with garlic. Mix rest of ingredients in small bowl to make a sauce. Broil shrimp 5-7 minutes or until pink, basting once with olive oil to keep them from drying out. There is no need to turn the shrimp. Do not overcook them. Remove from oven, drizzle with lemon sauce, and serve.

# Crab or Lobster Rolls

*If you live on the coast like I do, fresh crab or lobster meat may be available in your supermarket. If money is no object, treat yourself to a summer supper of these. Keep additions to a minimum, to enjoy the full flavor of the seafood.*

12-14 oz. fresh, already cooked crab or lobster meat
1-3 tsp. lemon juice or vinegar
Mayonnaise to taste; start with 1 Tbs. and add from there
2 stalks of celery or scallions, finely diced (optional)
Salt and pepper to taste
4-6 hot dog rolls
3 Tbs. butter, softened

Rinse crab or lobster meat and squeeze out excess moisture. In bowl, mix seafood with a bit of good quality mayonnaise, a dash of salt and pepper, and a little lemon juice. Add finely chopped celery or scallions if desired. Butter outside of hot dog rolls and grill on a skillet until toasted. Mound seafood mixture in rolls and serve.

# Barby's Scallops

*My childhood friend, Barbara Nash, is a corporate executive who occasionally gets to vacation at her family's island in Maine. Here is a dish she made for us on one of those trips.*

1 1/2 lbs. scallops
6 Tbs. butter, melted
2 tsp. minced garlic
1/3 c. white wine
Juice of one lemon (about 4 Tbs.)
1 c. seasoned bread crumbs
Salt and pepper to taste

Preheat oven to 350°. Pour half of butter in bottom of an oven-proof casserole dish. Top with scallops. Sprinkle lightly with salt and pepper. Spread with minced garlic. Pour lemon juice, wine, and rest of melted butter over scallops. Top with seasoned bread crumbs. Bake 20 minutes at 350°, or until scallops are tender.

# Shrimp with Snow Peas

*Not cheap, unless you prepare the shrimp yourself. But then again, it wouldn't be as quick as this is. You can also stir-fry the shrimp with the tails on and let each diner cut them off at the table. This dish cooks in 5 minutes once you have the ingredients assembled.*

1 lb. medium to large shrimp, shelled
8 oz. snow peas or sugar snap peas
1/2 c. chicken broth or bouillon
1/2 tsp. corn starch
3 Tbs. oyster sauce (available in gourmet section of supermarket)
2 tsp. cooking sherry
1/4 c. vegetable oil
1 tsp. minced garlic
1/2 tsp. powdered ginger or 1 tsp. minced fresh ginger
3 c. cooked rice

Stir broth, cornstarch, oyster sauce, and sherry in a small bowl. Heat oil in wok or skillet over high heat. Stir-fry garlic and ginger 30 seconds. Add shrimp (tails on or off) and stir-fry 60 seconds or until pink and cooked through. Remove shrimp to plate. Stir-fry snow peas 2 minutes. Add broth mixture, lower heat to medium, and cook 2 more minutes, until slightly thickened. Return shrimp to wok and heat through. Serve over rice.

# Cheesy Tuna Noodles

*Kid-friendly food, ready in ten.*

1 16-oz. box spiral pasta
1 can condensed cheddar cheese soup
1 9-oz. can tuna fish, drained
3/4 c. sour cream
1 chopped green pepper (optional)
1/4 c. chopped onion (optional)
Pepper

Cook pasta in boiling water. Add green pepper and onion to boiling pasta water for the last 5 minutes. Drain pasta. Return to pot. Stir in undiluted cheddar cheese soup and sour cream. Mix well. Add flaked tuna fish. Sprinkle with pepper to taste. Reheat gently until heated through. Serve.

# Vegetarian Fare

Tips:

- Keep lots of varieties of already shredded cheeses in the refrigerator. A simple saute of vegetables, amply sprinkled with cheese and served over a grain, is a quick and delicious meal.

- Canned legumes such as black beans, chick peas, and kidney beans keep indefinitely in the larder and enhance many a vegetarian dish as well as provide protein.

- Eggs are elegant, easy, and nutritious.

- Pesto makes for a quick meal when combined with pasta and a few sauteed vegetables. It freezes well and defrosts quickly. Keep a container on hand. (Once upon a time you grew your own basil and made your own pesto....)

- Time-savers in the produce department include pre-cut winter squash and potatoes, cole slaw mix, vegetable medleys, and bagged salad greens. You will pay more, however, and may compromise quality a bit.

# Fast Feta Pie

*From Alison Harris: "Here's a fast one I whipped up last week. My husband loved it; the kids wouldn't touch it. So, make Mac and Cheese for them and Feta Pie for you. Serve with salad and bread, and maybe a glass or two of white wine."*

16 oz. ricotta cheese
1 10-oz. package frozen spinach, thawed (or use chopped fresh, briefly steamed)
1 Tbs. chopped garlic
1 c. crumbled feta cheese
3 eggs
1/2 tsp. salt
1/4 tsp. pepper
1 frozen pie crust, thawed

Mix first seven ingredients in a bowl until well blended. Pour into pie crust. Bake 50 minutes at 350° or until done.

## Mexican Potatoes and Corn

*A single platter is used for cooking in the microwave and serving. Credit goes to the Maine Potato Board for a basic recipe, which I have modified.*

1 10-oz. package frozen corn kernels, thawed
1 16-oz. can black beans, drained
3 scallions, chopped white part, or 1/4 cup chopped onion
1 1/2 lb. potatoes, scrubbed but not peeled and cut into half-inch cubes (or use already-cubed potatoes from a bag)
1 green pepper, chopped
1/2 tsp. chili powder
1/3 c. taco sauce or salsa
2-3 c. grated cheddar or Monterey jack cheese, or a blend

Mix scallions with corn and beans and mound in center of a large microwavable platter or casserole. Mix potatoes, green pepper, and chili powder in a bowl, then arrange around edge of corn mixture. Spoon taco sauce or salsa over all. Cover tightly with plastic wrap, turning back one corner slightly to vent steam. Microwave on high for 12-16 minutes, rotating platter halfway through cooking time. Let stand 1 minute. Carefully uncover plastic wrap. Stir gently to mix vegetables and sauce. Sprinkle dish with grated cheese. Microwave uncovered for another 30 seconds or until cheese is melted. Serve with freshly chopped tomatoes, extra salsa, sour cream, and a salad.

# Curried Cauliflower with Chick Peas

1 head cauliflower, trimmed and cut into half-inch pieces
1/2 c. chopped onion
2 Tbs. olive oil
1/2 tsp. cumin
2 tsp. curry powder
1 28-oz. can diced or plum tomatoes, with juice
1/4 c. water
1/2 tsp. salt
1/4 tsp. pepper
1 19-oz. can chick peas, drained
2 Tbs. lemon juice

In large skillet saute onions in olive oil. Mix in cumin and curry powder. Add cauliflower and saute 2 minutes. Add tomatoes with juice, water, salt, pepper, and chick peas. Cover and simmer 10 minutes or until cauliflower is tender. Stir in lemon juice. Serve over basmati rice with plain yogurt, chopped peanuts, raisins, or diced cucumber on side if desired.

## Sweet and Sour Lentils

*Lentils cook faster than other legumes and are high in protein. Try this for economy and efficiency. Although the dish takes more than 30 minutes to cook, the pot does not require much tending, so you can go off to do other things while it simmers. Serve over rice or couscous with a colorful side salad.*

1 1/2 c. lentils
2 1/2 c. water
1/2 c. chopped onion
1 red or green pepper, chopped
1/4 c. cider or wine vinegar
2 Tbs. honey
1/2 tsp. salt
1 bay leaf
2 tsp. basil

Place all ingredients in large saucepan with lid. Bring to a boil. Reduce heat and simmer, covered, 35-45 minutes, or until lentils are tender, adding a small amount of water near the end if necessary.

# Scrambled Tofu Sandwich

*Tofu, or soybean curd, is like a black hole for flavor; you really have to be generous with spices for it to taste like anything. Tofu also doesn't keep long if bought fresh unless you rinse it every day. But if you buy firm tofu in a tetrapack, it keeps on the pantry shelf for a long time and is ready to be used at a moment's notice. This quick recipe comes from Muriel Hendrix.*

1 block tofu, about 12 to 16 oz., cut in small cubes (You can squeeze the excess moisture out of tofu by pressing it between a folded dishtowel, but this is an optional step.)
2 tsp. minced garlic
1/4 c. diced onion
1 Tbs. vegetable oil
Seasonings of choice: 1-2 Tbs. curry powder, or 2 Tbs. tamari and 1 tsp. ginger, or an herb seasoning mix
Salt and pepper to taste
Pita, or another kind of sandwich bread

Saute garlic and onion in oil in skillet. Add tofu and seasonings of choice, and scramble until hot and flavors are melded. Serve in a sandwich plain or with lettuce, tomato, shredded carrots, and/or sliced bell peppers.

## Hummus

*This Middle Eastern bean dip is delicious, protein rich, and ridiculously easy to make. Serve with triangles of pita bread or baguette slices with cut-up raw veggies on the side. This is particularly nice in the summer, when it is too hot to cook. Add various cheeses to round out the meal. Here is one very simple version.*

1 19-oz. can chick peas
2 cloves garlic, peeled, or 1 tsp. minced garlic
Juice from one lemon, or 4 Tbs.
1/3 cup tahini (sesame seed paste)
1/2 tsp. cumin
1/2 tsp. salt
1/4 tsp. pepper

Blend all ingredients in food processor or blender until smooth. Add small amount of liquid from beans if needed.

## Cheese and Bean Quesadillas

*Okay, so it's fancy grilled cheese. It still tastes good and takes only 4.25 minutes to prepare, according to Leslie Hunt who fixes this on the nights she has to teach.*

1 small can refried beans or jar Mexican bean dip
1-2 c. cheddar cheese
6-8 flour tortillas
1-2 Tbs. vegetable oil

Spread flat tortilla with thin layer of refried beans or bean dip. Sprinkle with cheese. Fold in half. Cut this in two or three triangular pieces. Grill in oil in skillet until tortilla is crisp and cheese is just melted. Serve with chopped fresh tomatoes, sour cream, and guacamole if so inclined.

## Two-minute Guacamole

Mash together 1 ripe avocado, 1 Tbs. salsa, 1 Tbs. lemon juice, dash of garlic powder, and salt and pepper to taste.

# Boboli Pesto Pizza

From *Liz Pierson:* "*This is our new favorite quick dinner. The basic recipe comes from Angie Atkins, and I have no idea if she made it up or what its origin is. It's incredibly fast and simple — about 15 minutes from thinking you'll make it to putting it on the table — and good, too! You can vary this in many ways. For example, use feta cheese or fresh parmesan and any choice of veggies and/or meats.*"

One large Boboli pizza crust
1 Tbs. olive oil
1/3 c. pesto
1 large fresh tomato, sliced
1 large green pepper, cut as you wish
1 c. shredded mozzarella cheese
Black olives (optional)

Drizzle olive oil over boboli and then spread pesto across it. Top with sliced tomatoes, green peppers, cheese, and olives. Bake at 450° for 8-10 minutes.

# Spinach Rice Casserole

*Make extra rice some night you are serving a different dish and use the leftovers for this.*

3 c. cooked rice
3 eggs, slightly beaten
1 lb. cottage or ricotta cheese
1/2 c. sour cream
1 10-oz. package frozen spinach, thawed and drained
1 tsp. basil
1/4 tsp. nutmeg
1/2 tsp. salt
1/4 tsp. pepper
1-2 c. shredded cheddar cheese

Preheat oven to 350°. Mix everything except cheddar cheese together in a bowl and pour into 9- x 13-inch oven-proof greased casserole dish. Sprinkle top with cheese. Bake uncovered 30 minutes or until firm.

# Black Bean Chili

*This is a favorite in Barbara Nash's household. Serve plain or over pasta or rice with a dollop of sour cream. Put leftover chili in a flour tortilla, top with cheddar cheese, and heat in the microwave for a nice lunch.*

2 onions, chopped
2 tsp. minced garlic
1 Tbs. vegetable oil
1 14-oz. can diced tomatoes, with juice (or use diced Mexican tomatoes and omit or decrease next 3 spices)
2 tsp. chili powder
1 tsp. oregano
1 tsp. cumin
1 can corn, drained, or 1 8-oz. package of frozen corn, thawed
2 16-oz. cans black beans, rinsed and drained

Saute onions and garlic in vegetable oil in skillet. Add everything else. Simmer 5-10 minutes.

# Thai Peanut Noodles

*This looks like a lot of ingredients, but once you dump them in a saucepan and heat the mixture up, you are done.*

12 oz. linguine or angel hair pasta, or rice noodles
1/2 c. finely chopped onion
1 tsp. minced garlic
2 Tbs. vegetable oil
1 c. chunky or smooth peanut butter
1 1/2 c. water
1/2 tsp. powdered ginger or 1 tsp. finely chopped fresh
1 Tbs. tamari or soy sauce
1 Tbs. cider vinegar
1/4 tsp. cayenne pepper
Salt to taste
1 Tbs. sesame oil (optional)
1 Tbs. honey or molasses (optional; taste your sauce first. If you use a sweetened peanut butter, you may want to omit.)

Cook pasta or noodles according to package directions. Saute onion and garlic in oil in a large saucepan. Mix in everything else. Heat to bubbling. Stir well. Turn off heat. Serve over cooked pasta or noodles garnished with a bit of chopped fresh greens, such as parsley, cilantro, or scallions.

# Garbanzo and Couscous Bonanza

*Garbanzo beans are chick peas. This chick sure likes how versatile they are. Here is one supper option, ready in fifteen.*

3 c. cooked couscous (Check directions on box. Couscous usually takes only 5 minutes.)
1 tsp. minced garlic
1 green or red pepper, chopped
3 stalks celery, chopped
1/2 onion, chopped
1 c. chopped carrot
3 Tbs. olive oil
1 15-oz. can garbanzo beans, drained
2 Tbs. lemon juice
1 tsp. each dried dill, parsley, and basil, or 1 Tbs. of each fresh herb, chopped
1/2 tsp. salt
1/4 tsp. pepper

Put couscous up to cook. Saute garlic and vegetables in olive oil in skillet until vegetables are tender but not mushy. Add everything else, stir, and heat thoroughly. Serve over couscous, garnished with lemon slices and fresh parsley if desired.

# Vegetarian Mexican Casserole

*Simple to assemble and bake. The perishable ingredients keep for a while, and the non-refrigerated ingredients can be staples on the pantry shelf.*

5-6 large flour tortillas
1 16-oz. can black beans, drained
1 14-oz. can diced tomatoes, drained
1 Tbs. finely chopped onion
1 tsp. minced garlic or 1/2 tsp. garlic powder
1 c. cottage or ricotta cheese
1 c. sour cream
3/4 c. salsa
1 egg (optional)
2 c. mild or sharp cheddar cheese

Preheat oven to 350°. Mix beans and tomatoes. Stir in onion and garlic. In separate bowl, mix cottage or ricotta cheese, egg, sour cream, and salsa. Rip 2 or 3 flour tortillas into bite-sized pieces and place on bottom of greased shallow casserole dish. Layer half of bean mixture, half of cottage cheese mixture, and 1 cup cheddar cheese. Repeat layers, finishing with the cheddar cheese. Bake 25 minutes or until heated through and bubbly.

# Greek Bow Tie Pasta

*We like this right after it is assembled and slightly warm, but you can serve it at room temperature or make it ahead and refrigerate it to serve as a salad.*

1/3 c. olive oil
Juice of one lemon
1 tsp. minced garlic
1/2 tsp. dried oregano
1 Tbs. chopped fresh mint or 1 tsp. dried mint
Salt and pepper to taste
12 oz. bow tie pasta, cooked, drained, and slightly cooled
1 red onion, chopped
1 red or green pepper, chopped
1 cucumber, pared and cut into cubes
2 stalks celery, sliced
8 oz. feta cheese, crumbled
1 4-oz. can sliced black olives

Combine first six ingredients to make a dressing. Cook and drain pasta. Rinse pasta with water to cool slightly, or let it sit while you prepare vegetables. In large bowl, toss cooked pasta with rest of ingredients and dressing. Garnish with quartered tomatoes and serve with greens and a crusty bread dipped in olive oil.

# Nice Rice Pilaf

*From Steve Van Savage, who does all the cooking in his house. Wife and writer LC Van Savage is one lucky lady. For extra protein, stir in chick peas or black beans.*

1 small onion, diced
2 Tbs. olive oil
1 c. basmati rice, uncooked
2 c. water
1 bay leaf
2 tsp. curry powder
2 carrots, diced
1/2 c. raisins
1 Tbs. parsley flakes or 1/3 c. chopped fresh parsley or cilantro
1 Tbs. dried basil
1/2 c. pine nuts
3/4 c. canned legumes, such as chick peas or black beans, drained (optional)
Salt and pepper to taste

Saute onion in olive oil in saucepan. Add rest of ingredients except legumes. Bring to a boil. Lower heat and simmer 15 minutes or whatever cooking time is recommended for the rice. Stir in legumes. Cover and let stand 5-10 minutes. Fluff with fork and serve with plain yogurt on side.

# Zucchini with Pizzazz

*A dish that takes minutes, because the slicing is easy and the zucchini cooks in no time. Serve over couscous or rice with a generous helping of freshly grated parmesan cheese.*

4 small to medium zucchini cut in quarter-inch slices
1 onion, thinly sliced
1 tsp. minced garlic
3 Tbs. olive oil
Salt and pepper to taste
1/2 tsp. each of basil, thyme, and rosemary
1 fresh tomato, chopped (optional)
1 c. parmesan cheese

Saute onion and garlic in oil for 3 minutes. Add zucchini and toss. Add seasonings. Saute on medium low heat for 5 minutes, adding optional tomato for last 2 minutes. Don't overcook, or squash will be limp and tasteless. Remove from heat. Sprinkle with parmesan cheese, toss again, and serve over couscous or rice.

# Soups, Assemblages, and Other Stuff

Tips:

- Half the battle in assembling dinner is being flexible and knowing what items go well together. Keep track of your successes.

- Soups do not have to be complicated or take long to prepare. When accompanied by a sandwich, salad, or crusty bread, they make for very satisfying suppers.

- Who says leftovers are no fun? Several of the following recipes are vehicles for smaller, leftover portions of this and that.

- Think outside the box. Yes, you can have pancakes for dinner and feel good about it too.

# A Sheet of Super Supper Sandwiches

*Say that five times fast.*

Use a big cookie sheet with sides. Take a large loaf of Italian bread. Cut it in thick slices. Spread one side of bread slices with a little olive oil. Broil until slightly toasted. Turn. Prepare other sides with one of the following combinations, depending on what you have on hand. Broil until cheese melts. Eat with a knife and fork if necessary.

- Mexican bean dip, sliver of red onion, slice of green pepper or avocado, tomato, sharp cheddar cheese.

- Olive oil, garlic powder, slice of avacado, slice of red onion, tomato, Swiss cheese or provolone.

- Olive oil, green or red pepper, tuna fish without mayo, tomato, mozzarella or cheddar cheese.

- Pesto, chicken or turkey pieces, tomato, mozzarella cheese.

- Apple slices, thinly sliced red onion, cheddar cheese.

# New England Fish Chowder

*A bowl of this 20-minute "chowdah" is a blissful supper, especially if served with blueberry muffins. Be sure to use whole milk or cream at the end, for a full bodied soup.*

1 onion, chopped
3 Tbs. butter
4 c. chicken or vegetable stock
2-3 potatoes, cut in small cubes, to make about 2 cups (I don't peel them. You can also use ready-to-cook potatoes from a bag.)
1 lb. chowder fish or haddock, cut in large chunks
1/4 tsp. pepper
1/2 tsp. thyme
1/2 c. cream or whole milk

In a large pot saute onion in butter for 3 minutes. Add chicken stock and potatoes. Boil uncovered 5-7 minutes. Add fish, lower heat, and simmer for another 5 minutes or until potatoes are tender and fish is easily flaked. Break up fish a bit. Stir in pepper and thyme. Add cream or milk. Heat through just to a scald, but do not boil. Serve topped with croutons or a sprinkling of chopped parsley.

# Polenta Lasagna

*Polenta is Italian cornmeal mush. It can be made from scratch or a mix or found ready to go in a tube shape in the health food section of the supermarket. Taffy Field's favorite quick recipe uses the tube kind. This is very easy to put together and tastes fancy.*

Basic ingredients:
1 tube ready-to-use polenta
1 28-oz. jar of your favorite spaghetti sauce
2-3 c. shredded cheese of your choice

Optional ingredients: cannellini (white kidney beans) or black beans, spinach, other vegetables, leftover chicken, etc.

In bottom of a greased shallow casserole dish spread half the jar of spaghetti sauce. Top with half-inch slices of polenta. Add a layer of canned beans, leftover chicken, fresh spinach, or cut-up veggies. Add a cup or so of cheese, another layer of polenta slices, the rest of sauce, then more shredded cheese. Bake at 350° until bubbly, about 30-40 minutes.

# Chicken Soup a la Rami

*Rami is our Israeli cousin who visited us after finishing a stint in the army, where he learned to cook this hearty soup. There is nothing exact about the proportions, so experiment away. Rami doesn't chop anything beyond quarters, which certainly makes this a seat-of-the-pants supper. The soup became very popular on a ski trip our family took with him. It is fabulous reheated; we all clamored for the leftovers. This serves 6-8.*

1-2 lbs. chicken parts, skin on or off, boneless or not
6 cloves chopped garlic or 2 Tbs. minced garlic
2 Tbs. olive oil
1-2 Tbs. paprika
3-4 potatoes
2 onions
1 bag of vegetables for soup, found in the produce section of supermarket. This bag usually contains carrots, a parsnip, celery, a turnip, onion. Or buy items individually.
2 Tbs. dried dillweed or a big bunch of chopped fresh dill
3 or more chicken bouillon cubes
Salt and pepper to taste

In large soup pot saute garlic in olive oil for 3 minutes. Add chicken pieces to pot and brown briefly. Add everything else, cut in half or quarters. Add water to just cover vegetables. Bring to a boil. Simmer uncovered about 40 minutes, or until chicken is done and the vegetables are tender. Add salt and pepper to taste.

102

# Cottage Cheese Pancakes

*These pancakes are high in protein and are particularly good with applesauce and cinnamon sugar. They are kind of like blintzes but far easier. Serve carrot and celery sticks on the side. A treat for supper!*

2 c. cottage cheese
4 eggs, lightly beaten
1/2 c. flour
1/4 tsp. salt
1/2 tsp. vanilla
2 Tbs. melted butter
Vegetable oil for griddle

Mix all ingredients except oil to make a batter. Heat oil on a hot griddle or in frying pan. Drop about 1/3 cup of batter for each pancake onto griddle. Fry until golden brown on one side; flip over and fry until browned on the other side and cooked through.

## Smashing Potatoes

*Put some muscle into your meal. Genie Wheelwright got this idea from some Swiss friends. It's a favorite at her house.*

Boil or bake a bunch of large whole potatoes, any kind, any size.

Put toppings you have in the refrigerator into little bowls: broccoli, bacon, chopped hard-boiled eggs, grated cheese, yogurt, sour cream, salsa, leftovers, etc.

Each diner grabs a potato, smashes it, and piles on whatever strikes his or her fancy.

# Minestrone Soup

*The vegetables can be varied; there is no science to this. Just use plenty of whatever you have on hand. For vegetarians, omit bacon and use vegetable stock.*

1 onion, chopped
1 tsp. minced garlic
2 Tbs. olive oil
1 quart low-sodium chicken, vegetable, or beef stock
1 green or red bell pepper, chopped
2-3 c. shredded cabbage, or use cole slaw mix from a bag
1-2 c. chopped carrot, celery, zuchinni, or summer squash
2-3 c. cubed potatoes, or use already cut-up potatoes from bag or 2 c. uncooked pasta
1 14-oz. can undrained diced tomatoes or 4-5 fresh tomatoes, chopped
1 15-oz. can white kidney beans, also known as cannellini
1/4 tsp. black pepper
1/2 tsp. each basil, oregano, and bay leaves
4 strips bacon, cooked and crumbled for topping
Croutons and parmesan cheese for topping

Saute onion and garlic in olive oil in large soup pot. Add everything else but beans and bacon, and simmer until vegetables are cooked, about 20 minutes total. Stir in beans and heat through. Serve soup topped with parmesan cheese, croutons, and/or crumbled bacon.

## Sweet Scramble

*Nothing wrong with scrambled eggs for dinner. Try these twists on an old favorite.*

6 large eggs
1 Tbs. honey
1/4 tsp. salt
2 apples, peeled and grated
1 Tbs. butter
1 Tbs. vegetable oil
1/2 c. cheddar cheese

Beat eggs with honey and salt. Heat butter and oil in a skillet to a sizzle. Pour in egg mixture. Stir until eggs are almost set, about 3 minutes. Stir in grated apple and cook until eggs are done, about another minute. Sprinkle with cheddar cheese and let cheese melt. Serve on toast.

## Savory Scramble

Prepare eggs as above, omitting apples and honey and adding pepper to taste. When eggs are almost set, stir in one diced tomato and 1 Tbs. pesto. Top with 1/2 c. mozzarella or parmesan cheese.

# Wrap It Up Supper

*An assemblage from Muriel Hendrix. Be creative with this.*

6-8 flour tortillas
3 c. fresh vegetables of your choice
1 Tbs. minced garlic
Salt and pepper to taste
2-3 c. cheese of your choice
Edible odds and ends

Steam, microwave, or saute with garlic one or more of the following: broccoli, spinach, Swiss chard, cauliflower, green beans, carrots, onion until tender. Sprinkle with salt and pepper. Place vegetables in tortilla. Top with lots of cheese, roll up, and heat in oven a few minutes, until cheese is melted. Other options: spread tortilla with some mayo or mustard and include in your wrap a slice of red onion, some leftover chicken, sausage, tofu, tuna, or anything else you find in the refrigerator or pantry that seems a likely candidate. Let diners create their own wraps. Heat thoroughly and serve.

# Tortellini Soup

*Some kids just love those filled pasta rounds called tortellini. Here's a soup that's almost as fast as any instant product.*

1 quart low-salt chicken, vegetable, or beef broth
2 c. cut-up vegetables
1 14-oz. can diced tomatoes with juice (optional)
1 8- or 9-oz. package tortellini — any variety you like, from the fresh pasta case
Herbs of your choice (optional)

In a large saucepan combine broth and vegetables. Simmer until vegetables are almost tender. Add tomatoes if desired. Add tortellini and boil for the length of time instructed on package. Add a sprinkling of herbs such as basil, tarragon, parsley, or oregano if you like. Shake in some salt and pepper if needed. Serve topped with shredded cheese and croutons, or plain for the kids.

# Ahead of the Game Salad

*A summer meal to make the night before, so you can watch Junior's entire baseball game.*

1 bag torn lettuce greens
1 15-oz. can chick peas, drained
1 pint grape tomatoes
1 large can tuna fish, drained, or 2 c. chopped deli meat: turkey, ham, etc.
1 red or yellow pepper, sliced or chopped
Thin slices of red onion
1 c. bottled ranch or other creamy dressing
1 c. shredded cheddar cheese

In large salad bowl, preferably glass, layer first six items in order given. Spread dressing in a layer over the top, right to the edge of the bowl. Cover bowl tightly with plastic. Chill until ready to serve, up to 24 hours. When ready to serve, add cheese to top and toss the salad. Serve with a good loaf of bread.

**Mexican variation**: Substitute black beans for chick peas and shredded deli roast beef or leftover beef taco filling for tuna fish. Mix 1/4 c. salsa with 3/4 c. ranch dressing. Proceed as above.

# Tomato and Mushroom Frittata

*Say "ta-ta" to dinner woes with this easy, omelet-like dish. Experiment with different vegetable fillings.*

10 eggs, beaten
1/4 tsp. salt
1/8 tsp. pepper
1/2 tsp. each basil and oregano
2 Tbs. olive oil or melted butter
1/2 onion, thinly sliced
2 tomatoes, chopped
1 c. mushrooms, sliced
1 c. parmesan or cheddar cheese

Preheat broiler. Whisk eggs in a bowl with seasonings. Heat oil or butter in a large skillet that can go in the oven later; a cast iron skillet works well. Add onion to skillet and saute until almost tender. Add mushrooms and saute 3 minutes. Add tomatoes and saute 2 minutes. Pour egg mixture into skillet. Cook, stirring slightly, until bottom is golden brown and mixture is partially set. Place skillet under broiler until the top sets. Top with cheese and return briefly to broiler until cheese melts. Cut frittata into wedges to serve.

# Split Pea Soup with Kielbasa and Potatoes

*If you plan to be out only half the day, put up this hearty soup before you leave. Use a crock pot on high setting only for this soup (low setting will not work) and come home to dinner, baby. You do have to soak the peas overnight, but no rinsing or draining is necessary.*

1 package green split peas (about 2 c.)
7 c. water
1 Tbs. beef, chicken, or vegetable bouillon granules, or use 3 cubes
2 tsp. minced garlic
1 onion, chopped
3 carrots, chopped
1 bay leaf
2 c. cubed potatoes
1/2 lb. turkey kielbasa or good quality hot dogs, sliced
Salt and pepper to taste

Before you go to bed, place split peas and water in crock pot to soak overnight. Next day, add everything to peas and water except kielbasa. Cover and cook on high for 3-5 hours. Give it a good stir when you come home. Add kielbasa or hot dogs to soup 10 minutes before serving and heat through.

## Summertime Express Lane Assembly

*We are not talking rocket science here.*

1 whole, cooked, hot rotisserie chicken from deli counter
1 bag salad greens of your choosing
1 pint grape or cherry tomatoes
1 box croutons
1 bottle of ranch or Caesar dressing

Place salad greens on individual plates. Slice warm chicken and place over greens. Circle plate with grape tomatoes, or cherry tomatoes cut in half. Top all with croutons. Drizzle lightly with dressing to taste. Voila.

Other additions (but not all at once): sunflower seeds, chopped hard-boiled eggs, shredded cheese, shredded fresh basil or parsley, cut-up roast beef or ham, sliced colored peppers, artichoke hearts, capers, chick peas, or what have you.

# Mom's Corn Chowder

*Yummy comfort food on cold nights. This is so simple my mother makes half the recipe for a quick lunch.*

3-4 potatoes, peeled and cubed
1 large onion, chopped
2 large cans creamed corn, about 15 oz. each
1 small can kernel corn, about 8 oz.
4 c. milk
6 strips bacon, chopped
1 tsp. dried rosemary
Pepper to taste

Boil potatoes and onion in large saucepan of salted water. Cook until potatoes are tender. Meanwhile, microwave or fry bacon until done, then chop coarsely. Drain cooked potatoes and return to saucepan. Add corn, milk, rosemary, bacon, and pepper. Heat to a scald and serve.

# Okay, Just Fake It

From LC Van Savage: "The easiest way to put dinner on the table is to just get a frozen thing and put it in one of your own baking dishes and reshape it a little and add a couple of things and screw it up a bit. Afterwards, make sure you destroy the evidence. I usually carry the empty frozen dinner boxes under my car seat and throw them into a dumpster behind a store on the edge of town at night."

# Oh, No! They Want My Cooking!

## What to Do When the Outside World Asks for Your Food

Tips:

- When it comes to appetizers and desserts, two popular "can you bring . . ." items, don't panic. Just about everyone welcomes something that is tried and true, especially if it turns out to be delicious and satisfying. Bring a dessert you're comfortable preparing or purchasing, without apology, and enjoy yourself. A friend of mine knows a nearby restaurant famous for its garlic knots, and that is what she contributes to every potluck she goes to.

- Garnish away for appearance's sake. A plate of store-bought crackers with a fancy cheese or two looks great with a few sprigs of heathery cilantro or scallion stalks tucked alongside. Add a ring of grape tomatoes and a sliced yellow pepper to complete the primary colors.

- Buy smoked fish or seafood or shrimp from the fish department, insert toothpicks into bite-sized portions, place on tray surrounded with crackers (or not), garnish with parsley and lemon, and there you have it.

# Bake Sale Solutions

*There is a bake sale at school tomorrow and your little
pumpkin has signed you up for cookies. Don't panic. Here's
what to do. (Or have Pumpkin do it.)*

## Oatmeal Chocolate Chip Cookies

Prepare one box chocolate chip cookie mix as directed on
package. Before baking, add 1/2 tsp. pure vanilla extract,
1/3 c. quick cooking oatmeal, and 1 Tbs. water to mix. Bake
as directed. Guaranteed to taste homemade.

## Chocolate Cookies

*No cookie mix in the house? Try these chocolate cookies
from a cake mix. Heloise shared this method in her
newspaper column.*

Preheat oven to 350°. Empty chocolate cake mix into large
bowl. Add 2 eggs and 1/2 c. vegetable oil and nothing else.
Mix well. Mixture will be stiff. Drop teaspoonfuls of
dough onto ungreased cookie sheet 2 inches apart. Flatten
slightly with fork. Dust with sugar or add a few colored
sprinkles to the top. Bake 8-10 minutes. Let cool 1 minute,
then remove from sheet.

# One-bowl Chocolate Chip Butterscotch Brownies

*A childhood favorite. This requires no rolling, refrigerating, dropping, or shaping. Just mix and bake.*

1/4 c. butter
1 c. brown sugar
1 egg
1 tsp. vanilla
1/2 c. flour
1 tsp. baking powder
1/2 tsp. salt
1 c. chocolate chips

Preheat oven to 350°. Microwave butter in bowl until melted. Add brown sugar and mix well. Stir in egg and vanilla. Add flour, baking powder, and salt and mix well. Fold in chocolate chips. Spread in 9- x 9-inch pan and bake 20-25 minutes.

# Snickerdoodles

*Even in the most limited of pantries you'll probably be able to scrounge up the ingredients for Snickerdoodles.*

1 stick butter or margarine, softened
3/4 c. sugar
1 egg
2 c. flour
1 1/2 tsp. baking powder
1/2 tsp. salt
1/2 c. milk
1/2 tsp. vanilla
2 Tbs. sugar mixed with 2 tsp. cinnamon for topping

Preheat oven to 325°. Beat butter and sugar until creamy. Add egg. Mix flour, baking powder, and salt together thoroughly. (I don't know about you, but I hardly ever sift anything first.) Add vanilla and milk to butter mixture. Add mixed dry ingredients to this and stir well. Drop by teaspoon onto baking sheet, sprinkle tops with cinnamon sugar, and bake 15 minutes.

# Quickest Fruit Cobbler

*A basic and delicious dessert to take other places or serve at home warm with vanilla ice cream. This serves four to six but can be easily doubled by using twice the proportions and a 9- x 13-inch baking pan.*

1 c. flour
1/2 c. sugar
1 tsp. baking powder
1/2 tsp. salt
1/4 c. butter, melted
1/2 c. milk
1 c. fresh or thawed frozen fruit, such as blueberries, sliced strawberries, raspberries, or chopped and peeled fresh apples; or pie apples, cherries, peaches, or blueberries from a can
2 Tbs. cinnamon sugar (1 tsp. cinnamon to 2 Tbs. sugar)

Preheat oven to 400°. Mix first four ingredients. Add melted butter and milk. Pour batter into greased 8- or 9-inch square pan or pie dish. Top with fruit. Sprinkle fruit with cinnamon sugar. Bake 30 minutes or until a toothpick inserted in center comes out clean.

# Tortilla Spirals

*You're supposed to bring hors d'oeuvres to a dinner party but haven't got time to fuss. Try these attractive, simple-to-assemble tortilla spirals. Thanks go to Lynn Heinz, who probably could make soup from a stone.*

1 package 6-8 large flour tortillas, plain or seasoned
2 8-oz. containers whipped cream cheese
1 bunch fresh basil
2 jars roasted red peppers
Parsley for garnish

Take a tortilla from package. Spread a layer of whipped cream cheese across entire tortilla. Down the middle lengthwise make a single row of fresh basil leaves. Next to that make a row of coarsely chopped roasted red peppers. Roll up tortilla. Do this with several tortillas; you may not need to use them all. Chill. (This is an optional step.) Just before serving, slice in one-inch lengths, making pinwheels. Place on tray surrounded by parsley. Aren't you clever.

**Other delicious fillings:** Smoked trout, cream cheese, and fresh basil (my favorite); cheddar cheese and bean dip; chived cream cheese and diced tomato.

# Pesto Dip

*Another super easy appetizer to get you out the door.*

2 Tbs. pesto
8 oz. sour cream
8 oz. small curd cottage cheese
3 drops Worcestershire sauce
Tomatoes for garnish
1 large baguette, sliced, or plain bagel chips

Blend first four ingredients together, garnish with tomato slices, and serve with baguette slices or bagel chips. Save leftover pesto for supper another night, or freeze.

# Chocolate Mousse

*A submission from Ellen Walsh. This dessert is so simple and so good, I had to include it. Besides, chocolate is the perfect ending to just about everything, isn't it?*

1 6-oz. package semi-sweet chocolate chips
1 egg
3/4 c. hot, almost boiling milk

Put chocolate chips in a blender. Add egg and scalded milk. Blend 30 seconds. Pour into small dessert dishes and refrigerate. Serves four quite well.

124

# INDEX

Beef Stroganoff, Sort of, 44
Cheating Jambalaya, 38
Half-hour (or Less) Chili, 42
La-de-dah Lamb Stew, 46
Miami Beef, 37
One-skillet Supper, 40
Pork Chops with Lemon and Thyme, 47
Pork Chops with Orange Sauce and Orzo, 48
Quick Beef Stroganoff with Sour Pickle, 35
Roast Beef Crostini, 39
Sweet and Sour Beef, 41

## Pasta
Angel Hair Pasta with Bacon and Peppers, 54
Bernie's Favorite Pasta, 60
Broccoli and Garlic Pasta, 58
Elbows with Creamy Pea Sauce, 55
Fancy Ramen Noodles, 63
Linguine with Clam Sauce, 52
Linguine with Turkey and Portobello Mushrooms, 57
Melissa's Famous Kielbasa Pasta, 64
Penne with Tomato Cream Sauce, 53
Pesto and Feta Pasta, 51
Rigatoni with Roasted Vegetables, 61
Take-along Casserole, 62
Tomato and Garlic Pasta, 59
What's in the Pantry Pasta, 56

## Fish and Seafood
Baked Sole with Parmesan, 71

Barby's Scallops, 76
Broiled Hawaiian Fish, 68
Cheesy Tuna Noodles, 78
Crab or Lobster Rolls, 75
Emily Swan's Easy Fish Fillets, 69
Fish Plaki, 70
Fish Tacos, 73
Greek Shrimp, 74
Lemon Pepper Fish Baked in Foil, 72
Shrimp with Snow Peas, 77
Spicy Fish, 67

## Vegetarian Dishes
Black Bean Chili, 90
Boboli Pesto Pizza, 88
Cheese and Bean Quesadillas, 87
Curried Cauliflower and Chick Peas, 83
Fast Feta Pie, 81
Garbanzo and Couscous Bonanza, 92
Greek Bow Tie Pasta, 94
Hummus, 86
Mexican Potatoes and Corn, 82
Nice Rice Pilaf, 95
Scrambled Tofu Sandwich, 85
Spinach Rice Casserole, 89
Sweet and Sour Lentils, 84
Thai Peanut Noodles, 91
Vegetarian Mexican Casserole, 93
Zucchini with Pizzazz, 96

# ORDER FORM

Use this order form to obtain additional copies of this cookbook or go to our website at www.ziplinepress.com. Thank you for your order.

Please send _____ copies of *Seat-of-the-Pants Suppers* @ $11.95 per book plus $3.00 shipping and handling per book to:

Name_____

Street Address _____

City, State, Zip _____

(Maine residents add sales tax.) Mail your completed form with check or money order to:

**Zipline Press**
**P.O. Box 622, Brunswick, ME 04011**

NOTE: We will be happy to gift wrap and send a copy of this cookbook anywhere in the USA. We will also include a small gift card. Add $3.50 per gift book to your total above. Please print your message clearly on the line below:

_____

Please send gift cookbook to:

Name _____

Street Address_____

City, State, Zip_____